DISCOVER YOUR TRUE WORTH

Awaken and Discover Your True

Worth as a Woman

Printed in the United States of America

First Printing, 2019

ISBN 9781070319506

Joanna L. Esparza

Email: joannal.esparza@gmail.com

www.joannaesparza.com

DEDICATION

To the girl, teenager, woman, mother, and wife, this is for you.

I dedicate this book to all the women in the world. Make your story count.

Armando, thank you for your patience, support, and the times of encouragement when I needed you. To my beautiful children, Alina and Josiah, I hope that I inspire you to change the world and find the boldness and courage to never back down from pursuing your dreams.

Don't let anyone look down on you because you are young, but set an example for the believers in speech, in conduct, in love, in faith, and in purity.

1 Timothy 4:12 (NIV)

NOTE TO MY READER

Have you ever faced rejection in pursuing your passion? How about fear before you even taking the first step? Do you doubt if you are capable of doing great things? I want to share with you my journey of tackling and overcoming rejection, fear, doubt, insecurity, barriers, and much more!

As a young woman trying to launch an organization while balancing life, family, work, and all the in-between, you can still take action and believe in yourself.

It's not easy, but it's worth it!

Because you got this

TABLE OF CONTENTS

INTRODUCTION

Broken. Afraid. Alone. Insecure. Uncertain. Lost. Unworthy. Not enough.

Can you relate? This is how I felt as a teenager. Even today, there are times when I still feel this way. Why? Well, let's just keep it real; the struggle is real! Every day, we wake up and make so many decisions. It feels like we are making about 100 decisions a day! What am I going to wear? How will I do my hair today? What's for breakfast, lunch, or dinner? Just think about it. We keep going, going, and going! It's never-ending. The reality is that we need to just stop, take a breath, and relax - take a minute to invest in ourselves. If we do not take the time to invest in ourselves, we will be run by everything and everyone else. Take a moment to just breathe, read a book, listen to a podcast, sit down with your life coach, or better yet, pray! Whoo yes. Just pray! It has taken me awhile to get comfortable with sharing my background and story. Though I chase my dream and I am living part of my dream, I hid tremendously behind the scenes. I hid because I did not want to be the center of attention or bring much attention to my past. Call it what it really is; SHAME. It was scary! I realized that it is my past and the past stays behind me. Our past does not determine who we are. What we really need to focus on is our future. I took control over my past, and I used my experiences, my story, and the vision I had to create a message to the world.

That message is that I am Worthy, I am Fearless, I am Bold, I am Unique, and I am Enough!

Guess what?

So are YOU.

#shebecame209

Grab a pen, highlighter, journal, and make sure to answer the questions at the end of each chapter.

PART 1
AWAKENING

CHAPTER ONE: OUR POWER

Acts 1:8 (NIV)

*"But **you will receive power** when the order Holy Spirit comes on you, and you will be my witnesses in Jerusalem, and in all Judea and Samaria, and to the **ends of the earth.**"*

We truly don't realize the power we have until we recognize the power God has given us. Our life is full of events, stories, and experiences that can change a life. Sadly, many of us do not reach the point of realizing how powerful we are.

That was me. I did not tap into the power I had complete access to until my early 20's. It was then when I began to discover my limitless potential that I have and can achieve. I am a firm believer that our life has a great purpose and that we were not created just to survive, but also to live. To live a life reaching our true potential and discovering why we were put on this earth. For many years, I felt a void in my life. There was a part of me that felt empty, and I knew that something was missing. My natural instinct was to look for ways to fill this sense of emptiness. As a teenager, you really do not hear how wonderful, beautiful, capable, or worthy you are. Or at least I didn't. Come to find out, that affected me as a young woman. It affected my self-esteem, confidence, and my belief in who I was. Not knowing my worth and not knowing who I was cost me many mistakes. Mistakes that I am not proud of. I became a girl who craved attention from the wrong people. I sought self-assurance in others when really I should have had the self-assurance in myself. I am sure that I am not the only one who has dealt with that issue and it makes me wonder. I wonder how many more young women have also experienced something similar to what I did. I wonder what their lives look like today and which direction their lives are taking.

Just imagine for a moment our girls growing up knowing how loved, valuable, and important they are to our world. That they have a place and a voice in this world. I look back at my childhood and the days in which I was in Junior High and High School; I wish that we had more activities, clubs, or programs that would remind me and instill these crucial values into my heart. I believe that having those seeds planted inside of someone can make a huge difference.

What can we do in life without knowing who we are and having a solid foundation to keep us rooted? We cannot deny that our children are being influenced by their peers. Whether it be positively or negatively, they are being influenced. That includes today's music and their lyrics, music videos, movies, news stream, and social media. I am sure that I don't have to go into details, but I would like to entertain the social media subject a bit.

It has become extremely easy for our youth to access pornography, nudity, sexting, I mean our children have never been so exposed to this until this era. It's terrifying! I am shocked when TV shows slowly and discreetly hide messages that I surely do not want to pass down to my daughter. However, our control is very limited now. To be honest, I was also exposed to all of this at a super young age, and I can see it growing immensely. Why is our focus shifting to this? I completely disagree and am totally against it! How our poor children are struggling more than ever with insecurity, identity issues, comparison, addiction, etc., can we just take a moment to think about how things would turn around if we shifted our focus into raising confident, determined, and strong kids? That our children would be our main focus in nurturing them with love, respect, values, support, and encouragement. That's what we need more of! To be honest, I think if I had a little bit more empowerment and encouragement growing up as a teenager maybe, just maybe, I would not have made so many mistakes. But it is those mistakes that have shaped me and have made me who I am today. I realize now that my life has power and that power has always been there, but I didn't take full advantage of it. With that awareness, I now have the freedom to decide if I will use this power or keep living a life powerless. Will I choose to use the power I have complete access to and use it to impact, influence, and transform our generation? I do not want to live a life regretting that I never spoke up or tried to help anyone. I wanted to use my story as a tool to help transform lives. If I could help just one person or hundreds, I would.

I don't want to be the person on my deathbed regretting that I didn't do anything to help make this earth a better place and not use my time I was given here on earth.

In Acts 1:8 we are told that we will receive the power when the Holy Spirit comes upon us. The Holy Spirit will come and you will be a witness to all the ends of the earth.

Take a moment to think about this for a minute.

Once you have the power of the Holy Spirit, God will use you, your life, and your voice to be a witness to the ends of the earth. It is a promise, and the Word of God is never void. He has already spoken this, all we have to do is accept and welcome the Holy Spirit in. You can be used in mighty ways in your lifetime. Your life has incredible value, and there are people who need what only you have to offer. Consider this an invitation in discovering who you can become and who you can impact through the power of God.

REFLECTION:

Has someone shared with you before that there is power in your life and in your voice?

_____

_____

_____

Do you wish to learn what that power is and how to tap into it?

_____

_____

_____

If you answered yes, I would like you to take this opportunity to invite God and the power of the Holy Spirit into your life.

Lord, thank You for dying on the cross for my sins. Forgive me for my sins and come into my life. Lord, I thank You for the gift of the Holy Spirit. Holy Spirit, I welcome You into my heart. I ask that You live inside of me and I permit You to take over my life. Use me and my life as you wish. Give me the confidence, strength, and boldness to keep on going. From this day forward, I will live a spirit-filled life. I will count on You for support, advice, and wisdom. Allow me to hear the voice of God and understand the things I can not. Give me eyes to see what You see. In the name of Jesus. Amen.

If you prayed this prayer, you have just begun a new journey in your life! It is an exciting one, so be ready!

CHAPTER TWO: OUR NEED TO LOVE

A s a little girl, I was blessed and fortunate to have both my mom and dad in the picture. My father owned his own welding business, which kept him away most of the time. He would stay in the bay area during the week and come home only on the weekends. Therefore, I mostly lived with my mother. Growing up, I was not able to connect with my mom. I felt as if she was always physically there, but never emotionally there. I missed the feeling of being able to connect to that motherly love and warmth only she could offer. With my experience, I can tell you that being emotionally available for your children is more important than physically being there. Why do I say this? Being emotionally there for your children and how you raise them will build their character and nurture them to become tomorrow's leaders.

If our children lack love, self-esteem, and self-worth, the most valuable piece in their life is now missing when they become young adults.

Something will always be missing because that need was not filled. It creates a void inside of us that was intended to be filled. We were created to love and to be loved. In John 13:34, we were commanded to love one another. Each person has different ways of receiving and giving love. It's important to learn the love language of others, especially those around you. Most importantly, this also includes your spouse and children. I encourage you to look up the different love languages that there are and begin to implement them into your life. I assure you that you will start to see love and service in another way. It may help in your home, work, or in the way you do community. I will be sharing with you about an organization that I began, and I promise you that I didn't put two and two together until a few months ago. I discovered that I was using my primary love language to be the main message of this organization.

Words of Affirmation. I began using words of affirmation to send out our message to girls, young ladies, and women with I AM CARDS. They were cute business card sized cards that said: *"I am Beautiful, I am Loved, I am Unique, I am Free, I am Fearless, I am Strong."* The response was HUGE! I slowly began to hand out these cards everywhere I went. Whether it be starbucks, stores, offices, even cars! If I had the opportunity to give out a card, I did. You should see the faces of those who picked up that card and just read it. It was as if their face just lit up! Their spirit and confidence had just been fed. That is because most of us don't tell ourselves how amazing, wonderful, beautiful, or strong we are as often as we should. Instead, we compare ourselves, tear ourselves down, or even degrade ourselves before speaking positivity. The Bible tells us that our words have the power to speak life or death and that our tongue is like a two-edged sword. There you go! There is one of the answers to the many problems we are facing now. We lack in the use of positive words towards each other. We hold a valuable answer to many of our problems, and the best part is that it does not cost us anything! Only perhaps some training and practice in changing our vocabulary and actions towards each other. Maybe, just maybe, if we used our words to build each other up, we would have more confident, strong, loving, and empowered women! If this is you, and you are already someone who speaks nothing but positivity to build others up, kudos to you! Thank you!

#CHOOSE2BEE

If not, let's take this moment to shift our focus and make a pledge to #choose2Bee. That means you will Build, Empower, and Encourage others. Get it? B.E.E. It's catchy, isn't it? This pledge is a super important part of the making of this book because it's an awakening in the need to love, encourage, empower, and build others up daily. Each day we encounter someone and we may not know what they are facing in their lives. However, we have the power within ourselves to show patience, kindness, love, compassion, gratitude, and positive affirming words. A simple smile can change someone's day. It is your smile that can make an impact on someone around you. I encourage you to become more aware of your surroundings and those you have access to. That can be your kids, parents, neighbors, coworkers, your local barista, and extended community.

I have a story for you that confirms what I have just said. A few years ago, I attended a training in the bay area. It was after hours, and I decided to go to the stores. I wanted to drive, but I felt the need to take a walk instead. I came to a red light while I was looking down at my phone browsing my Facebook page. Suddenly, I noticed from the corner of my eye a driver calling the person next to me over to give her some change. The girl that was next to me was a young lady. She must have been in her late teens or no more than 21 years old. I took a few minutes to talk to the young lady, gave her a donation, and lastly, I asked her if I can pray for her. I began to pray over her and tell her how valuable she was and the tears started flowing down her face. I guess that through all the struggles, trials, and tribulations she faced, perhaps these words have not been spoken over her in some time. This must have touched her deeply, which caused the tears to easily flow out.

If it was not for the red light and the driver who singled her over, I would have kept walking across the street and would have never noticed her. This shows us how easily we are distracted by technology, ourselves, and everything else around us. I encourage you to adopt a new way of thinking; be willing to be interrupted throughout your day to stop and listen. You never know who God has aligned you to cross paths with. This very story has impacted my life and I share it over and over to let others know that it's important to be available for others.

We need to listen, encourage, and motivate others. The same goes for us; we need this too.

You were made to love and to be loved

REFLECTION:

Considering that we each grew up completely different but share similarities ...

Describe your childhood in the space provided.

_____

_____

_____

I want you to write down how your parents raised you, nurtured you, and your home life.

_____

_____

_____

Next, I want you to think about your friends, interactions, and experience in school.

_____

_____

_____

What were your friends like? Were you bullied, positively influenced, etc.

_____

_____

_____

Take this moment to just breathe. If there are any painful moments, stay with me. I promise you that there is a point of why I am taking you down memory lane.

If there was an ah-ha moment in this chapter for you, write it down in the space below.

_____

_____

_____

_____

_____

_____

_____

_____

_____

_____

_____

_____

_____

_____

_____

_____

_____

_____

CHAPTER THREE: OUR SPIRIT

Jeremiah 29:11

The Lord knew you before you were even born and before you formed the shape of a human. He already had you planned. He knew exactly who you were going to impact and what you were going to do in this world. He knew each day of your life. He saw it way before you ever did. I was now a teenager suffering from an identity crisis, and I had an emptiness inside of me from the lack of feeling loved. I searched in all the wrong places to feel loved and accepted. I searched for validation and security. I searched and searched, but I kept falling short. I would get my cup half full only for it to soon be empty again. One way that I was trying to fill up my cup was by dating around. The only thing that my soul searched was for someone else to make me feel like I was someone important. I wanted to be seen. I wanted to be known. I wanted others to see me for me. I can't even believe what I am describing right now. I was a teenager! A teen girl searching and needing for their love tank to be filled. I can take a look back now and realize what a mistake I was making, but at the moment, it was not a mistake. At the moment, it was my way of surviving. This attention that I craved so much, I needed to keep going. What do you think happened after so long? I gained a horrible reputation. One that I am not proud of. One that I was trapped in, and I began to claim as my very own identity. This label was planted so deep in my spirit that I began to claim it in my life.

How many of us have been called names or been told that we are not good enough? Then we suddenly begin to make those labels define who we are. We allow them to stay in our lives, and we give them a space to occupy in our minds. As long as they remain in our minds, they will remain in our hearts. If you are in a place where you are trying to get your cup filled and you are searching in the wrong places, let me tell you that you can begin to find fulfillment and begin to feel loved today.

Discover your identity in Him.

You will find love and self-love by first knowing who created you, why you were created, and the purpose for which you have been created. Jeremiah 29:11 tells us that the Lord knit us together in our mother's womb, AND before our body formed a human shape, He already knew the plans He had for us. Before we even knew it, we were chosen and selected to be someone important here on earth. That only tells us that we have immense value to this earth. This is because we were not created by accident, but by a divine purpose and mission. Our life has incredible value, and it is up to us to discover the purpose as to why we were created. However, life will throw us into the fire to try and destroy that incredible value that we have. It begins at an early age with our identity and confidence, and if the lies and the trials of life knock us down before we even try to get up, then we have already lost the battle. But if we stay strong, firm, and rooted our in identity and purpose, there will be nothing to keep us from reaching our full potential. I had heard this scripture many times, but I allowed the distractions and the lies to deter me from what was ahead of me. I was worried more about the now and the today vs. keeping my eye on the prize. I did not value the prize at the moment. It could be perhaps that it was not something tangible that I could have had then. So, instead, I attempted the shortcuts in life. Though those shortcuts are not really shortcuts, I made my life more complicated and added a few more chapters in my book.

Taking that into consideration, it was a good thing. It now gives me a few more life lessons to share with you.

I am sure that you, or perhaps someone you know, may have also experienced something similar to this. I will share with you that the relationship I had with my father was absolutely amazing. Though he was away most of the time, he was not absent. He was my biggest cheerleader in all of the dreams I had as a little girl. He was funny, encouraging, loving, and available when I needed him. My father suddenly passed away in the fall of 2012. I cannot begin to tell you the pain that I experienced during this season of my life. I felt like my world had just ended.

No one is ever prepared for the loss of a loved one. I had just turned 20 a few months back, and all I knew was to rely on my dad for emotional support. My father was my backbone. I relied on him for support, love, advice, and encouragement. When he passed, I had to learn how to rely on my heavenly Father. The Father who is always there, no matter what. The one who sees, clothes, provides, and never forsakes you. He was now the only father figure I had in my life. I realize now, that I had to experience the loss of a father in order to seek Him and begin the real journey of pursuing His love. If I had not lost my dad, I would not have had an awakening of searching who I really was. It was a new season for me, and it was time to begin what was going to be a long season of a few years of recovery and discovery.

My spirit had awoken and the transformation process began. All things happen from a seed. Whether it be an idea, a dream, or a human, there was a seed in place. Over our course of life and in the current season we find ourselves, there are seeds that are being planted in us. Perhaps, some seeds have already been there and depending on where you are or who is in your life those seeds may be receiving the nutrients they need.

Those seeds are being watered and nurtured to begin flourishing. Well, do those seeds sprout suddenly after just one watering? No. Each day, little by little, they are receiving what they need. You and I are both receiving, each day, what we need to get to where we are going. Believe it or not, this very life you are living has been pre-planned and written out. We can continue to go on this path either owning our calling or completely denying that we were called for such a time as this. We will each come to a day or a life event in which we will have an awakening inside of us to make a shift. This shift will set our life course in the direction of realizing our giftings and limitless potential. My awakening began with the loss of my dad. Yours can very much look similar to mine or may be completely opposite. Either way, I want you to know that it is time for your spirit to be awakened. When your spirit is awoken, you should be in alignment with who you are, your purpose, and your passions. It is then when you wake up from your day to day sleep and begin to live and thrive vs. living and surviving.

REFLECTION:

Do you feel like you are living and surviving or living and thriving?

_____

_____

_____

Have you taken the initiative to discover your purpose in life?

If so, what is your purpose in life?

_____

_____

_____

If not, take a moment to answer the following questions.

If I had the opportunity to either volunteer or to start a new career, it would be...

_____

_____

_____

What is preventing you to pursue this opportunity?

_____

_____

_____

Whatever you just wrote, throw it out the window!

It is what is stopping you from fulfilling something that will take you from surviving to thriving!

Do not let fear, limited beliefs, or doubts keep you down any longer!

CHAPTER FOUR: OUR WORTH

I was on my way of discovering who I really was and the value that I had. But first, let me share with you some key things I had experienced so that you can get an idea of some of the major struggles I dealt with inside. I was sixteen when I first met my husband, and I was living on my own. At that time, I was living a life that I should not have been — doing things that were above age appropriate — engaging in a party lifestyle — consuming unhealthy things that were damaging my body. Not to mention illegal. Let's just say that I was not respecting my body either. In the last chapter, I shared with you briefly of the void I was trying to fill. Well, here goes nothing. Here comes the cry of an unhealthy, wanting, and hurting teenager. Meeting my husband couldn't have happened at a better time. The way I was going, I was destined to fall in the wrong hands. Without a doubt, I know that the Lord sent him into my life to redirect me. However, I was in for a surprise in the next few years. The first couple of years were difficult! Gosh, they were difficult and long! I fell in love at a young age. I gave it my all in this relationship. At my most vulnerable stage in life, I believed in the words he told me, and I trusted him. For the next year, I lied to my parents about where I lived. They were under the impression that I was staying with a girlfriend. When in reality I was living with a man that whole year. Everything was good, or so I thought. I thought he was madly in love with me and that I was the only person in his life. But I was mistaken.

During the early years of our relationship, I allowed verbal abuse to be very common in our relationship. I thought it was okay at the time. It seemed normal, I guess. I allowed it from the way we communicated. Little did I know what I was doing to myself. I discovered betrayal. I discovered infidelity. Not only once, but a few times. I chose to be blind and to forgive. The sweet moments, the sweet words, and the great makeup sex covered up my feelings. I was burying my feelings that I just didn't want to deal with. I didn't want to recognize them. I chose to bury them under the rug. I chose to believe that things were okay and that I was okay. When was it going to be enough for me to believe all of the lies about myself, or to allow someone to live a double life only so that I can feel safe? I was letting the words of a man and the feeling of being safe in my life to rule, which brings us to a realization about women. We will allow things that make us feel "safe" dominate our happiness and our freedom! I want you to think about your life. Think about that "safe" feeling in your life. What is that one thing that makes you feel safe and inside your comfort zone that you are willing to put down yourself and your freedom to keep it alive? For me, it was a relationship. A toxic relationship that included infidelity, verbal abuse, and betrayal. It was these things that tied me down and kept me away from my destiny. I had permitted insecurity, doubt, and lies to dominate my life. They had so much power over me that I didn't even know who I was anymore. I was buried under false beliefs and accusations. Now, I am not totally blaming this on a man. This was me too. I permitted the lies to dwell in my mind. To repeat themselves over and over until I became those lies. I questioned myself and kept asking myself what was wrong with me. I would compare myself to others in the hope that I would find what I was missing that the other person had. I couldn't stop all of these doubts in my mind. They controlled me and practically tortured me. It's important to realize that we allow this. We allow these thoughts to control our mind. We let them inside, and we let them live inside of us when we should be taking full control of our thoughts. The Bible teaches us that we have the power to take every thought captive. So why don't we? We have to become stronger, and we have to love ourselves. YES, love ourselves. Know ourselves and our most inner being. We need to be kinder to ourselves and build ourselves up. If you don't love yourself, then how will anyone love you? Or how will someone get to know you properly if you don't even know yourself? How will anyone respect or care for you if you don't respect and care for yourself?

Women, I am telling you that you have to know your worth! You have to know that you are loved! That you are valuable! You have to know that you're beautiful and unique! That you were created for a higher purpose.

You, my love, you are worthy, loved, unique, beautiful, strong, fearless, amazing, and powerful!

Just in case you have not heard that in a while, go ahead and read it again. Read it as many times as you need to.

I want you to know that you are loved and you are so special! That truth will help you so much in life and in the moments when you feel defeated. As for me, it took me a while to believe this truth, and it may be the same for you. But it's one of the most important relationships that we need to fix. It's the one with ourselves, so we can then work on the relationships with our partner. Keep in mind that great relationships don't happen overnight. I had to do a check-in on myself and realize who I was. I had to figure out my purpose and why I was created. I went back to a point in my life where I still felt okay and in my safe zone. That was when I still had my dad in my life. It was before all of the confusion in my identity and the awareness of a void I had. It was before the labels and lies began to pile up. It was before all of the gossip and misguided friendships. If it's something my dad lived for, it was for me to know God. He made it his mission to guide me to the Lord. There was a time in which my husband, who at the time was still my boyfriend, and I had separated, and it was in those moments that something drew me back to the Lord. It was those seeds of faith that were planted in my early years. I went back to church and began to fill the emptiness I had inside. I started to remember my worth and of who I was. It was those very seeds that were planted inside of me for a reason. Just as I shared earlier in this book, some seeds are being planted in us. At any stage of your life, those plants may be getting nourished or simply will begin to sprout later on in life. I can tell you this for sure. No matter how small the seed, it will never be taken for granted. As I continued to dig deep within myself, I began to feel loved again.

As I slowly began to fill my heart up with love, fulfillment, and purpose, I became a different person. I was now allowing those seeds of faith and truth to begin getting watered inside of me. I wanted to see more fruition in my life. The person I was becoming was stronger and it was noticeable. It was noticeable because I, as a woman, began to set limits and boundaries in my life. I began to demand to be treated with respect and dignity. No longer was it okay to treat me like an emotional doll. I was a human being, and most importantly, I was the daughter of the Most High. We are the daughters and creations of the highest. This was an awakening so deep inside of me that it fueled my most inner being. It's a super exciting feeling that I had, but it's not quite easy for me to describe on paper. However, you would think that by this time, I had a little bit more guts not to fall back. I didn't. I fell back into old habits a few times. It was actually a few times. Transformation doesn't happen overnight. Healing doesn't happen overnight. I can tell you what does happen overnight - seeds are planted. The emotional healing of women is a process. My own healing took over a year. Over a year to get in a good place. Happy to be my own internal and external me. At that time, I used my local resources and began to see a professional counselor. I met with her a few times. I had some ah-ha moments. But can you believe it? I still went back. While all this is going on and my emotions and confidence were worse than a rollercoaster, my relationship with God was continuing to strengthen. So at this point, you may be thinking, "When is enough, enough?" Well, that looks very different for all of us. My enough was when I reached a point where I was full enough to say NO MORE. No longer will I allow inappropriate jokes or NO longer is it okay to use negative words towards me.

This is where I began to demand respect. I asked to be treated as if I were a child of God. Because that's who I was. I had to believe this at my core before I asked it from someone else. I also had to treat myself with respect so that others will as well. I finally began to believe it and to live in a way to honor myself, and it's a good place to be. It's a good place to know that you are loved, valued, and created for a purpose. That you are not here for a reason or are an accident. You are a precious addition to this world. You can become who you have been made to. It is you that can turn any negative experience, thought, belief, or lie into something positive and turn it into a weapon and a tool to impact others! Now is your time. This is when you wake up! This is when you put your sword up and fight like a warrior!

REFLECTION:

As a woman, do you feel as if you are living a life in which you value yourself and your worth?

_____

_____

_____

_____

Have you always known your true worth as a woman?

_____

_____

_____

_____

List how so, or the time in your life when you didn't, and things turned around for you.

_____

_____

_____

_____

CHAPTER FIVE: OUR VOICE

Mark 5:19 (NIV)

Jesus did not let him, but said, "Go home to your own people and tell them how much the Lord has done for you, and how he has had mercy on you."

Daniel 4:2 (NIV)

It is my pleasure to tell you about the miraculous signs and wonders that the Most High God has performed for me.

I would like to explain to you how I was feeling in my life for a season. Though I began to learn again who I was in Christ, my marriage began to improve, and my family began to grow, I felt dry. I felt as if I were living, but only to survive. I was surviving, but I was not thriving. I felt as if I had to speak up. Here I go again on this search in life for answers. It was as if something or someone was calling me from a deep sleep. Passions, interests, and images were being stirred up inside of me. I began to dream. I began to have a desire. I began to listen to this desire of me becoming more than who I was. Let's back up for a minute and take a look at the order in which things happened. There was a spiritual awakening that took place before any of the work of healing began. I had to first awaken my spirit to come off the autopilot life I was on to then discover my worth. Once I began to discover my worth, the next phase began for me. That was the process of discovering my purpose. I had to know my worth and believe in myself before becoming who I was created to be. I remember coming across a post on Facebook. As I read, it touched my heart. It was an invitation for women who wanted more in life. Who searched for a sense of community and belonging. That was my first step to discovering what this desire and passion was inside of me that was being stirred up. I attended this meetup group held by a group of women and fell in love with the atmosphere. As I continued to participate in these meetups, I became more involved with this group. Relationships began to flourish. As I continued to attend this group, I had a growing sense of belonging, and it started to awaken a spark in my life. I decided to take things to the next level and began to see a life coach. I wanted more in life, and I knew I needed help in searching who I was created to be. My husband was never in agreement with me as I sought guidance and help from a life coach. He insisted that I connect with a Christian counselor or mentor. He believed in the ability the church had to help me discover myself. So I went behind his back and continued that path in seeing a life coach. I have to admit that though this life coach did help me realize incredible things about myself and also helped me resurface gifts I had buried under layers of limiting beliefs, fulfillment came from the Lord. In other words, my husband was right. Our true identity and our gifts come from the Lord. Life will take us through hurdles, detours, and obstacles to make us doubt ourselves and our abilities to thrive in life. It was a short time that I worked with my life coach. In this short time, believe me, it was enough to get me on a jump start to uncovering all my hidden and buried potential. The life coach I began to work with, along with the community group I was involved with, began to ask me questions that made me resurface passions that I had. These questions weren't so many things that I would hear or see at church. This is what, I would say, drew me out of the church to seek. The questions were: What are you passionate about? What is one thing that you would do if fear or failure were not an option? What is that picture that you keep visualizing yourself doing in life? Perhaps, this is something that you see more of now, but back then I, myself, did not. I absolutely fell in love with the feeling of just talking about these dreams. I was far from making them happen, but it felt so right. I felt a burning desire just to wake up in the mornings again and just dream. Dream as if I was a little girl all over again, and in my imagination, I could do anything and reach the stars. That's what I was doing. I was dreaming and reaching for the stars.

As I began to dream, I began to journal. I began to write down the visions and questions I had.

- What would you tell your younger self?
- What message do you want to send to the world?
- What do you see yourself sharing in life?

As I began to answer these questions, I was taken down to memory lane, and that was back to my Junior High and High School days. It was this that was burning in my heart. I had to tell both younger and older women that they were loved, beautiful, smart, talented, and enough! That they did not have to degrade themselves to try to fit in or allow anyone to tell them their worth. As if there was a desperate cry inside of me that was silently trying to come out. That was it. That was my message. I had just discovered my message, and learning to turn my message into my voice was an interesting life-learning season! Could I have said that any better? Was I naive and thought that it was going to be easy to begin this journey, better yet, have a positive response to what I was doing? Heck, yes! I did imagine a totally easy, positive, unicorn, perfect rainbow up ahead of me.

Imagine this: me crashing into a brick wall. That's what it felt like when I crashed into this reality: I am too young! In my opinion, the biggest lie we can face is 'I am not enough.' This lie is one of the deadliest and most dangerous lies to our spirit. If we entertain this enough, it will destroy us. This lie can become a reality for us if we let it. It's important to realize that this lie can keep us away from reaching our full potential. Being aware of its power works in our favor. This lie can come disguised in many forms. For example, I am not pretty enough, I am not smart enough, talented enough, light-skinned, tall enough, etc.

You are too young.

I dealt with the lie that I was not good enough because of my age. Over and over, I kept coming across this barrier of my age, and not until recently did I learn to publicly embrace the fact that I am young and powerful. Now, don't get me wrong, I knew inside that I was young and powerful, but publicly, I did not want to shout it out.

I did not want to tell people my age in the beginning. I wanted people to see me for my heart, passion, and actions. Why? Because once someone learned my age, it was like shooting myself in the foot. No matter what I would have said or created, the response was: oh, you're young, you have a lot to learn, or oh I am not taking her seriously because she's a millennial. So instead, I tried my best to keep this truth to myself and grounded myself to this scripture (1 Timothy 4:12). It kept rooted in times I needed it to. When this lie began to play in my head that I was not enough because of my age, I took refuge into the Word of God. Jeremiah 1:7 tells us (do not be afraid for I will give you the words to speak), and without a doubt, I knew that when I spoke, it was God. When I dreamed, I knew it was God. When I wrote, I knew it was God. It was all Him, including the making of this book. Just when I thought I gave it my all, I felt led to add more. This chapter is one of those moments in which I felt that I need to add this truth, that we need to embrace our voice and message at whatever age! Let us not be afraid because God is with us, and He will give us the words to speak when we need it - Luke 12:12. The Bible also teaches us not to be afraid because He will help us. He is always there, and He walks with us, no matter the situation.

So you're too young, huh?

Did it ever occur to you that being young was an advantage? It's an advantage because how many young folks are willing to pay the price at an early age?

How many young people are full of drive and ambition?

How many young people get shut down immediately and get a sour taste in their mouth that makes them give up right away? I can assure you the numbers are small in this case. How many adults tell us: "Well, I wish I would have started when I was younger." "If I knew what you knew at my age, my life would have been different." How about this one: "If only I had a mentor growing up." I have heard this from amazing people in the world, and if they would have a positive, uplifting, butt-kicking support team, this person would have blossomed even earlier in life.

Why not, instead of shutting us young people down, give us a chance. Yes, a chance! Why not take us under your wing and mentor, support, and build us up? Very few people are willing to invest, spend time, and train others up. I reached a point in my life where I did not want to share my age nor talk about it. I hoped for the age question not to pop up, and it did. It's something inevitable for some reason. When I was asked my age, I had no other choice but to tell the truth. I mean I was not going to lie about it. Though some people looked into my eyes and told me what a wonderful thing it was that I was young and what I was doing was great. Oh, and the famous line, boy I wish I started when I was your age, I would be in a different place right now. I observed how some people did not want to help me, and I felt the immediate disconnect after discovering my age. There I go, I continued on my path without them. Now, on the other hand, I experienced others telling me the same thing, but this time, it was different. Behind the words of encouragement and praise on being young, there was action. And if you know me, I am all about action. Young or old; it's about your actions, values, and beliefs. Ultimately, if you have it, then you're going to do it. Now I am not an expert at reading people, but I can totally feel when something is not right or simply not authentic.

Note to self: please be authentic!
Shout out:

I just want to shout out to the wonderful women out there who are super incredible by empowering and supporting others! It's incredible to see and experience your inner circle, and your close ones are completely authentic, super-empowered, and happy to see you succeed. This is whom you shall surround yourself each day, each moment, and each opportunity with!

My advice, don't waste your valuable and precious time on negative, nagging, no-dreamer, dream-killers that will suck the life out of you.

Learn to identify those who will help you and elevate you in life vs. the ones that will cause you to stay stagnant or sink along with them! In the Bible, we learn about the story of Joseph and the dream he had that one day, his brothers were to bow down to him. Well, his brothers were not happy about that dream. Instead, they became angry and eventually traded their own brother for silver. Joseph needed to safe-keep that dream to himself because of his own family; his own blood did not like that dream. But who were we to step in Joseph's shoes and know what he was thinking at the time? This story helps us and works in our favor!

Hunny, we learn to safe-keep that dream.

Guard that dream that you have, surround yourself with positive, believing, uplifting, and empowering individuals who will believe in you for who you are and for your passion, drive, and actions! Like I said, your actions! Let your yes be a yes, and your no is no. Live in a way that your character, word, values, and beliefs will show in your everyday life.

You have all heard it. You can tell the type of tree it is by the fruit that it produces. Keep in mind that people are always watching you and what you do. That means to watch your every move, social media post, words, activities, actions, speech, the friends you have, you name it, and someone is always watching. So guard yourself, your heart, and your eyes - the windows to your heart. Guard your heart so that when any lie, disappointment, disbelief, thought, or words come your way, you can shield them, and it will not penetrate into your heart. *Matthew 6:21 (NIV) For where your treasure is, there your heart will be also.* Whatever life - it may be a distraction or barrier - is in front of you today, give it to God! Let it go, and let God! You are a powerful human being with a valuable purpose here on earth. You are unstoppable in the eyes of God! Take control over your life and crush every negative thought by taking each thought captive! - You got this!

In what disguise has the 'I am not rnough' lie tried to bring you down?

_____

_____

_____

Now, tear this page out and throw it away in the garage!

Throw it out of your life and don't ever give it power!

Note:

If you are over the age of 30, I want to ask you a favor. Please give someone a chance who has shown you passion and drive. Work with them, help them, support them and, most of all, mentor them if you can. Even if it's for one coffee date. Your support and encouragement can go a very long way.

REFLECTION:

What burning desire do you have in your heart to pursue?

_____

_____

_____

If you had the opportunity to send out a message to the world, what would it be?

_____

_____

_____

CHAPTER SIX: OUR BELIEFS

I want to dedicate this chapter to you and what your beliefs are. We can have many limiting beliefs in our mind that are truly holding us back and keeping us away from what is in front of us. We could be just one step away from our triumph. So what are limiting beliefs? Limiting beliefs are things that we believe that keep us held back. It could be lies that we were once told or that our parents passed down to us. * *Limiting beliefs are just as they sound - beliefs that are limiting. It is something that sets a limit or boundary that you cannot look past. Picture yourself ready to run a race, you can see the track, and it's clear you have a clear path, but then when you try to take off there is a chain that has you by the ankles.

That chain is that limiting belief that is holding you back. While you can see what's ahead, while you can picture or dream what your future is like, this chain is strapped to you at the ankles keeping you back and not wanting you to run the race. So what will it take for you to break away from the lies, the heaviness of false beliefs, or the chains that are keeping you away from your happiness and living your best life? My advice - <u>turn those limiting beliefs into the opposite of what you have believed</u>. Exposing whatever it is that has you frightened, captive, and even living in fear will bring light into your existence!

Remember, darkness cannot live where there is light!

Your future is in your hands! It is you and only you that can turn your life around and give it purpose. Breaking away from those limiting and false beliefs will give you the strength to keep moving forward.

The truth is that you are a child of God. You are worthy. You have been called to be a prophet to the nations, and you have been SET FREE! You are free to dream, create, and discover all of your hidden potentials. So don't let anything keep you back. Don't let words, physical pain, or emotions be the reason that you are not reaching for the stars.

As I am writing this book, I currently work full time. I have a regular 40-hour job. I run a nonprofit that is rapidly growing. I am married, and I am a mother of two children — Alina who is 8 and Josiah who is 4.

I can't begin to tell you some of the things that ran through my mind or are still running through my mind.

I struggle with this daily.

- How am I going to do all this?
- What in the world am I doing?

Who in their right mind signs up to work, run a nonprofit, commit to monthly blogging, write a book in the midst of this, all while trying to keep my marriage healthy and be a good mom! Not to mention that I love serving! So attending Sunday services is a must, and volunteering at my home church is almost a must! Well, it's all because of passion! Once you get a glimpse of what you have access to, you will find the strength and endurance to overcome any lie, barrier, or obstacles that may come across your mind.

Every second, every minute, and every hour I had, I used to invest in writing this book.

Whether it be on my break, my lunch hour, before or after work, late nights, or early mornings, there I was trying to write this book. And not just write this book, but everything else in just mentioned that I am a part of. I was questioned many times how in the world was I able to do all that I do. If you look at my Facebook page, it was full of activities, but what many did not know is that behind closed doors, I was suffering. I was suffering from a chronic condition that was caused after being rear-ended. I was rear-ended in March of 2016, and then again in May, just two months later. I suffered and still suffer from Occipital Neuralgia, which is a pinched nerve and any sudden movement or sleeping the wrong way, being too active could practically paralyze me in pain. Yes, I lived through it, and I fought and continue to fight it. Though this was not a mental limiting belief, it sure was a physical limitation. It was like having a leash on. While I wanted to do so much more, many times I couldn't. Through the physical pain, I had to keep on going: waking up every day to go to work, to be there for my kids, to continue to advocate for She Became and still try to live a normal life.

I seriously had to take control of my thoughts, my body, and those limiting beliefs so that I could take control of my destiny. Your limitation can be disguised as physical impairment or mental state of mind. Trust me, it is a daily battle. A daily struggle, but your future is worth it. I was chosen to become one of twenty leaders in Northern California and the Central Valley to participate in cohort with some pretty powerful, incredible women who are changing the lives of girls and women. The craziest part is that I was rejected the first time. They were only going to accept 18 leaders. Somehow I knew that I was supposed to be a part of that cohort. I had given up hope since they offered me to be an "alternate participate" and that I would be notified within a certain date. Seriously, I had given up, and the lie played in my head that "I was not good enough."

As I kept my faith and I kept myself grounded each day affirming to myself that I was enough! That I was capable of great things and that I needed to keep moving forward, God was making a way! He was stirring up the hearts of the people who ultimately decide who will be a part of this cohort. I was chosen! The budget was increased to add two more participants! Nine days after the date I was given that I was going to be notified if there was room to add me, I received an email of acceptance!

Yes, I was doubting myself. Yes, negative thoughts crossed my mind, and YES did I think less of me! But you know what, as those thoughts came across my mind, I became the bigger person and threw those thoughts right out of my mind! I was at a point in my life where I was strong enough to overcome limiting beliefs, and like that, I knew there was still value in where I was at that very moment in life.

Perhaps you are at a point where you want to break free from all of the negative self-talk and start your journey in reaching your full potential. This is it. This is the moment that you have been waiting for.

Take a moment to pray about this. Bring it to God and give Him all of the junk that is weighing you down. Begin to turn around the negative into the positive.

REFLECTION:

Write down one negative belief that has been holding you back.

_____

_____

_____

_____

Now write down the opposite of that belief.

_____

_____

_____

_____

In the end, you only have yourself to pick yourself up. What is one truth that you can write down to lift you up in moments when you feel defeated?

_____

_____

_____

_____

PART 2
THE JOURNEY

THE MESSAGE

It was an exciting time for me at this point. I had embraced the fact that there was power in my voice and that I needed to use it. Little by little, I began to journal ideas, thoughts, and things that inspired me. One day, while I was on maternity leave, I had some extra time and found some crafts to work on. I painted a mason jar, added some glitter and totally glamified it! I had some amazing scrapbook paper and bam! I turned this jar into a gratitude jar and shared it on my social media account. From this beautiful creation came an exciting opportunity. I had been invited to be a guest speaker at a women's group. This was the same group I had previously mentioned where I began to awaken who I really was. I was full of excitement - and fear! This was the first time that I was going to speak in front of a group of women!

With the full support of my wonderful husband and the burning desire of speaking, I began the preparation. I put something together to share the reason I fell in love with gratitude and you know I had to mention my dad in all of this! I crafted up some beautiful mason jars, prepared the gratitude slips, and went all in! The day had arrived with 26 women waiting to hear my message. So there I go, terrified, but passionate. I shared my message, walked the ladies through making gratitude jars, and a spark was ignited in me in the summer of 2015! I knew it was because of the spark that I wanted to keep going. This was a feeling that needed to be in my life. I had never felt so alive like I had on this day! A new person had just resurfaced on this earth. Instantly, I knew that this was a new part of my life. I had to find ways to keep this flame alive. So that's what I did. This little mind of mine kept dreaming and dreaming. So many things I wanted to accomplish, yet so limited on resources. But that didn't stop me. I continued to listen to my heart and continued the search. By this time, I was actively becoming more and more involved with my community. I was now involved with two community groups for women and became close to someone whom I shared similar dreams with. We partnered up to host our very first vision board workshop for women. While we were at the facility getting all of the logistics for our workshop, I had bumped into an old colleague of mine. We were able to connect, and I was able to share with him our current project. That's when a door had suddenly opened, and I was about to begin walking through the door of opportunity. Only this time, it was one of the greatest connections and divine appointments in my life. I just didn't know it yet. What do you do when life gives you an open door or a window of opportunity? You take it! All of this positive energy and a girl with wild dreams was welcomed to come to speak to young women. This girl was needed to fill in the lack of motivation, self-esteem, self-love, and confidence in the girls. Are you beginning to see the connection now? If not, it's okay; we're getting there. By this time, I was at a point where I was hyped! Amazing things were going on. I had become more actively involved in another community organization that quickly became a huge part of my life. Why? It was a great cause! Empowering women and reaching women! It was right up my alley. It felt so right! My confidence was at one of its highest points in life. I had reached one of my long lost desires in life. To become more active in my community, build relationships, and impact the lives of women. In the next few months, I was going to experience a shift in my life that I did not expect. I was not expecting the transition, but my husband saw it since day one. Gosh! Don't you hate it when our husbands are correct? My husband knew that I was too involved and that I was not going to get anywhere doing what I was doing. I, on the other hand, kept going because I was filling up an area in my life that was much needed — giving back. I was giving back to my community and fulfilling a part of my purpose in life. I won't get into much detail on what happened next, but just know, life redirected me. I was redirected into something like solitary for the next few months. I was now battling confusion, doubt, rejection, and God knows what else. Things didn't work out as I thought they would where I was. That's when the search continued. If you thought I was dreaming before, then I was dreaming of reaching the moon at this point. In the winter of 2015 and the spring of 2016, I had taken things to the next level in my life. I had never been so serious about walking in my purpose until now. This girl was on fire and was ready to show the world what I had to offer!

REFLECTION:

I want you to take this chapter and let it inspire you to think about something that would absolutely bring you so much joy that you know deep inside that you have to continue to do this in your life to keep you full and content.

Use the following questions to help you discover what that might be.

What is that one thing that you most enjoy doing that had brought you so much joy?

_____

_____

_____

If you were not able to answer the question above because you were unsure, what do you think would be that one thing you would most enjoy in life that, without a doubt, you know would make a difference in your life?

_____

_____

_____

What is one thing that you can start doing today to begin a search or continue doing to ignite or keep that spark going in your life?

_____

_____

_____

THE BEGINNING

D o you recall in the last chapter that I shared with you that I had crossed paths with an old colleague of mine? Okay. Well, this person was the program manager over at a nonprofit organization that helps youth from ages 17-24. Project Yes helps both young women and young men with job placement, job interview skills, mentoring, tutoring, etc.

When connecting with the program manager, I learned that there was a huge need for encouraging young women in many areas of their lives. I learned that there is a huge number of homeless youth, foster care youth, youth that we were alone and sadly vulnerable. I now had an opportunity to become a positive role model for young women. So that's what I did. I became more actively involved with this organization, and I began to dream of ways to inspire, motivate, and empower young women. All while networking and starting to come out of my comfort zone, building and rekindling relationships. I had a name for this vision, but it was not perfect.

She Became

One day over a coffee, a colleague of mine had agreed to move this vision forward alongside me. We worked together in coming up with a new name for this vision. After brainstorming a few different options, we had come up with the perfect one. She Became! This name is powerful, and let me tell you why. How many of you are starting the journey of healing, transformation, or change with something negative? Perhaps, not something negative, but definitely not where we are striving for. Here's the perfect example: I BECAME FEARLESS! In the process of all of this, I had become a fearless person. A person who was not afraid to fail, did not give up, or quit when things became tough! Now, what can we say about all of the girls who will be impacted?

She Became ... strong, bold, resilient, confident - a doctor, an educator! Right! The possibilities are endless for us, and ultimately we have the decision to choose who we want to become.

So who will you become?

From a seed, a dream, a vision, a burning desire, to an actual organization! She Became was formed!

YES! I was given an amazing opportunity to launch She Became - a mentoring program at Project Yes. It was the summer of 2016 when I, along with two wonderful women, walked onto a school campus and introduced an opportunity of change, growth, and transformation to many. But it didn't come easy. We had chosen a demographic of girls who mostly did not believe in themselves, or did not want to engage in a program like this; perhaps they just weren't interested. Others had walls up, others were just too busy and distracted with other things in life. It was about one girl out of twenty that were really at a point where this was what they wanted! But yet, we still did not give up there. We continued, and we pursued them. That's what you do when you do things with heart, purpose, and passion!

Project Yes has been a huge part of my life. I owe much of my success to the program manager who believed in me.

All it took was one person

All it took was one person to believe. It took one person with faith, guts, and an open heart to give this girl a chance. It was 2016, and I was 23 years old. It was at age 23 when someone took a chance on me! From trial and error, the establishment of a program for young women was in the works. I can't help but just laugh at the craziness of what I was doing. I had no experience, no knowledge, and absolutely no clue how to run an organization, ler alone start one. But I did it. It was not easy, and I was not alone. Even though sometimes I felt like I was alone, I was not. I had a few cheerleaders around me, and I was determined to seek the help, guidance, and mentors that I needed to make this happen. So, that's what I did. I sought help, guidance, and mentors. Let me tell you that God will send you the right people in your life to walk along with you on this journey.

When I said yes, He aligned me with someone who would be a pillar to what was about to happen next. Our passion was like a consuming fire within us, and we worked. We worked endlessly creating material, content, and planning. Our passion will drive us to the end of the world. Passion will help us overcome fear, barriers, and all doubts. It's a passion that will give us the strength to keep on going when things seem impossible and take us many places. It will protect any dream and any vision that we have. So if you are passionate about something, then you have one of the key components to run with your message. If it's one thing that cannot be taught to a person, it's how to have the passion for a specific cause. Either you have it, or you don't. A manager once told me that what set me apart from all of the other interviews was the passion that I had! By now, you may know that passion isn't the only thing you need to become successful in anything. More than passion, you need people. The right people in the right place. That means whatever strength you lack, you need to find in others. The easy part is finding them. The hard part is finding the ones who will stand with you and who are prepared to overcome any challenge, put in the work, and buy into the mission. We hit a few roadblocks there. We thought we had some of the right people in the right seats, but we were not quite there. In the early stages, we had some adjusting to do, but after a while, we had the right people. After all, the ones who stay with you from day one and show their resilience are the ones you want right there next to you. I don't want this to disappoint you in any way. If you're in a place where you are working towards a goal and you need a team, but you don't have the right team members yet, I want you to know that it's okay. Pray about it, and in time, you will have them. I also don't want you to disqualify yourself if you lack knowledge in a specific area. That area will be filled! Girl, pray. Keep it in prayer, and the Lord will answer. Just keep going! Trust me; if it's a good thing, nothing will stop you from making it happen. Yes, you may be slowed down, but it will come to pass!

REFLECTION

Take this moment to think about some of the obstacles you had to overcome to pursue something you have desired.

_____

_____

_____

In the space provided, write down something you could have done to have had a better response OR something that you can do to get a better response.

_____

_____

_____

Next, write down an area that you need God to fill.

_____

_____

_____

Keep this in your prayers.

Write down the names of those amazing people who have kept you strong, encouraged, and are building you up each day.

_____

_____

_____

It's important to recognize the wonderful people that you have around you supporting you.

THE JOURNEY

Alright, so at this point, the journey had begun on building this program, and it was getting surreal. In this part of my book, I will be sharing with you some of the battles that I was fighting to keep things alive, strong, and positive in making this dream a reality. It was December of 2013, just one month after I had started a new job; my mother was diagnosed with terminal brain cancer. Almost two years after losing my father, I was now in the process of losing my mother. Her fight with cancer went on for two and a half years, and I was right there fighting with her. In March of 2015, we had our second child, Josiah. Let's do a little recap to make sure we understand this story to its fullest capacity. So I transition into a new job, my mother becomes ill, I get pregnant during this time, I have a baby, I have a call inside of me trying to surface, and I begin to search to fill this area in which I was feeling empty.

There is this shift in my life from late 2013 to about the mid-year of 2016, where God was preparing me and awakening me for the next season in my life.

I was on this journey of becoming the woman of God I was created and destined to be. Keep in mind that I had to share with you what I was going through to be able to share you with the journey of becoming who I am today. While my personal life was under attack and I was trying to create something beautiful, things didn't stop me there. My mom had GBM (glioblastoma), a terminal brain cancer. It's one of the fastest growing cancers someone can have. The mass she had happened to be on the right side of her brain, which affects her feelings, personality, and increases her sensitivity. That truly explained so many things about her behavior that many of us did not understand. I loved my mother very much and what this disease did was mend our relationship, grow my faith, and equip my endurance. The doctors had given my mom a 6-month life span and told us 10% of the people with this condition survive over two years. Well, my mom lived two and a half years with this type of cancer. She was above ten percent! It was a testing, painful, and beautiful battle in life. There were so many lessons, awakenings, and gifts in the battle my mom was in. As much as she was battling, we were too. My husband, our children, and our family. Let me take this moment to just give a huge shout out to my husband who played a huge role in this season. He was so encouraging and helpful at this time. Frankly, I owe much to him. There were many times when I had to be with my mom and take care of her, take time off of work, take her to doctor's visits, run to her rescue at times, etc., Let me tell you that in this season, I grew so much resilience in both my faith and my calling. I knew that I was being prepared and equipped to reach my full potential. Just as the emotional healing process of a woman does not happen overnight, neither does the process of discovering your life's purpose. It is a process. A process in which you will be tested, stretched, and forced to come out of your safe zone. Yep. We don't always want to be pulled out of or forced to come out of our comfort zone, but it's absolutely necessary to go through it and make it to the next level in life. During this storm, I journaled my feelings, questions, and new dreams that were being awoken. It was as if my pain was writing a story and helping me turn my pain into purpose. I began to write lessons, and they were beautiful! I had no idea that I had this gift in me. At first, I did not embrace them, so as I prepared them, they would stay on paper, and I would not share them with the public.

I began to use the cry I had inside of me to turn it into a message others needed to hear. And it was not just the pain I had, but also the words I would have loved to hear or learn as an individual. I was told by one of my pastors that I had a beautiful writing gift and that my style was very simple and easy to understand. That makes perfect sense! I am not much of a complicated, long reader, or an individual who goes on and on. I love getting to the purpose right away! Hearing this from a pastor gave me so much confidence, and it empowered me to have more confidence in myself!

Growth

As I continued to work, being a mom, wife, and the best daughter I could, She Became was becoming more and more recognized. As an organization that was becoming more recognized came more work! I then began to learn to juggle home, an ill mother, work, ministry, and She Became. Here I was, this passionate young woman with an incredible opportunity to bring something new and fresh into the lives of young women. I began to use the little resources (my funds) I had to share She Became. I introduced the program to a few people in the community, and I faced rejection in a lot of areas. Some of the feedback that I received was you're too young, go partner with your church or another organization that is doing something like what you're describing. Perhaps your vision is to be a part of the church? Hmm... well, do you know what I did with the feedback? I took it, but I didn't receive it. I knew that I had a vision that was bigger than me and I was not going to be stopped. I recognized that burning desire that I had, and I knew that I was not going to stop until I achieved what I strived for. Yes, I did face insecurity and disappointment. I thought that I would be welcomed with wide open arms and that it was going to be easy. Nope. It didn't happen that way. Things were difficult. With prayer and a surrounding team of incredible faith-believing perseverers anything was possible. We knew that She Became was something that was from above. I knew that God had trusted me with this vision and that we were going to go over the mountains to keep going. You know that when something good is in your hands, you're going to face opposition. You will have to fight for great things! She Became was flourishing and reaching more and more girls. One of the most important things that we had to do is prove that we were serious and that we were here to stay. We had to gain the trust of our community and its members. Slowly but surely, we were gaining ground in our community. However, things at home were becoming worse. My mother was becoming more ill, and my sister and I decided that it was best to have mom move in with her. Now I had added frequent visits to my sisters' house to help and support both my mom and my sister. My sister lived in Paradise, CA at the time and was about three hours away from my house. I had to leave both of my kids and my husband behind a few times in order to be of help to my mother and sister.

Thanks to my loving and supporting husband for always being so understanding. Thanks, Babe!

This was becoming very heavy on me, and it was becoming more difficult to balance work, marriage, kids, mom, and She Became. If it were not for prayer and faith, I would have quit by now. But I kept pursuing, remained grounded, and rooted in the Word of God. Stronger and stronger, my faith grew each day. I had so much faith and believed that my mom was going to get healed from this cancer. All meanwhile still trusting God and praying for His will to be done. It was until the last day I kept on having the faith of complete healing; I did not want to lose her. But I had a calming feeling that I was able to fulfill my duty as a daughter in the seasons she needed me while repairing our relationship and creating loving and long-lasting memories. I was at peace, and I felt that God was ready to take me to the next season of my life. She passed away, and peace had just taken over me. I knew that she was in a better place and it was time to focus on family, career, ministry, and the advancement of She Became. Amazing things followed. We now had a reputation of a great program for young women. We had proven that we had an amazing vision and our success stories began to increase. We now had some pretty amazing supporters that would just keep encouraging, guiding, and mentoring us along the way. It's so crucial that you find people who will believe you and support you along the way. Because we will never feel secure 100% of the time, and when we are doubtful, it's those positive people around you that will lift you up in the time of need. Today, I am surrounded by some of the most amazing people in my life. Truly, if it were not for them, we would not have gotten this far.

It was God

So how was I able to restore my marriage, keep my sanity when I lost both of my parents, juggle work, home, ministry, and the launch of a new organization? Yes, you answered that right. It was all God. We all have choices in life, and I could have easily kicked God out of my life and fallen into anger, depression, other spiritual rituals, but that was not for me. I chose to anchor myself in the Lord and His promises. It is a priceless feeling to have joy, peace, strength, and comfort in life.

I encourage you that whatever journey you are in, anchor yourself in the Word of God. He will show up, and He is never late! Everything will happen according to His will.

REFLECTION:

What is something that you faced or are facing in your current season?

_____

_____

_____

_____

_____

_____

Write down your current favorite quote or scripture that helps you in the time of doubt.

_____

_____

_____

_____

_____

_____

THE CALL

Wwhat will your life look like after reading this book? Perhaps, you have a dream that you would like to make a reality, but fear and doubt are stopping you from taking action. At the end of each chapter, I added a few reflection questions. If you took the time to complete the questions, you might have realized the connection in your life. You realized that each test, trial, and season had taught you something. Whatever that something is, you have the power to turn it around and make it loud with your voice. Make it loud and make it known! You are a very powerful person, and it is only you that can make the decision today to turn it around and turn it into a tool or weapon to impact others. You, my love, have a powerful story and it's not yours to keep inside. Take this time in your life to ignite that spark that you have inside of yourself and change the world! Change your world and what you believe in and change others around you with your beautiful story!

Remember that this is not about me, but this is about you! You have been called for such a time as this. You have been surviving for so long and have experienced success, trails, and opposition. It was in that exact season where God was shaping and molding you to become who He has created you to be. Before you knew it or before you accepted His call in your life, everything around you was preparing you for your future. I wanted to share some of my most personal and vulnerable stages in life to help you realize that there is power in each life event that we experience. I personally analyzed each remarkable event and have turned it around into a message that can change the life of someone else. That, by chance, it will INSPIRE YOU TO MAKE A DIFFERENCE IN YOUR HOME, WORKPLACE, COMMUNITY, AND WHO KNOWS PERHAPS EVEN HAVE GLOBAL IMPACT. Had I not chosen to take ownership and share these stories with you, they would have been for nothing. I did not want to come to a day, in which I'll no longer be here, and my story would never have had the opportunity to be shared with someone else. I wanted to dedicate my life story, experiences, struggles, and victories so that one day it will inspire someone to do the same. I am a firm believer in using our voice as a tool to impact others. In the next couple of pages of this chapter, I want you to think about your life and your stories and how you can turn it into your life's message. Remember that when you make this decision, there will be many trials to test your endurance. The moment that you decide to make this shift, you will have many open doors, and you will have opposition at the same time because that's just how life works. I didn't make the rules, but I have learned that our life here on earth is temporary and we need to make our time here count. Remember when I shared with you that I was living life, but I was not thriving? I want you to thrive in life, feel alive, and find a burning desire to keep you going each day. That each morning when you wake up, you feel inspired and happy to tackle what life throws at you. Happy to tackle on life? Say what? Yes!!! When you are secure and grounded into your purpose and God, yes God, you will find the endurance to keep going. As soon as I became aware of my gifts and said yes to my purpose, the dreaming didn't stop, neither did the opportunities. In the Fall of 2017, I was chosen and challenged to lead a ministry class for new believers and also to develop the curriculum. I had written small faith-based lessons but never a full curriculum. After a few months of hard work and dedication, I developed this curriculum for new believers, Shaped. Trust me, it was not easy! I faced some huge giants along the way. First, I was quite exhausted; developing a curriculum is challenging! I doubted myself and the ability I had to create something original, and I questioned myself many times, was this good enough? I would tell myself that this curriculum was about to be taught at one of the top churches in my area. What would others think? What would my pastor say? In the end, this curriculum needed to get approved before being printed by my pastor. The day came when I had to send it over for approval, and guess what? All of my doubts and insecurities were for nothing! Shaped was a great curriculum! It was simplified and relatable to new Christ followers. Just what I was asked to do and what I was able to deliver! Now, for this book, you can't imagine how many times I read this book over and over to make sure that it was good enough. Eventually, I reached a point where I accepted what I had created and gave myself the approval that I needed to say, "Okay, this is the best."

This is my story, and this is what I have to offer.

She Became Campus Program

She Became then became a regular program at a college campus, it was then welcomed into our local school districts reaching Junior High Girls, and more opportunities came with the office of education. It came to a day where I really had to choose between what I was going to keep moving forward with. Why? Well, it had become too much to continue balancing work, family, Shaped, She Became, and my writing.

Overcoming

As I continue to overcome limiting beliefs and a physical limitation I do not allow it to control my life, nor do I allow it to give me false hope. Instead, it has only slowed me down. I may be slowed down, but never shut down! I want to encourage you to also adopt this way of thinking. Don't let your limiting beliefs or physical impairments keep you away from what God has for you!

The Ant Philosophy

So you have excuses, huh? My list could have been very long, but instead, I chose to look at those excuses and turn them into learning lessons. Have you heard of the ant philosophy? It goes like this: *If ants are headed somewhere and you try to stop them, they'll look for another way. They'll climb over, they'll climb under, and they'll climb around. They keep looking for another way. I have been able to adopt this philosophy and make it part of my life. I will always look for a way to make things happen.* - Jim Rohn

I will find my place back on track! That's the mindset that you need to have!

My Prayer

I pray that nothing holds you back from achieving your dreams or any goals. Let it not be a physical condition, lack of resources, fear, doubts, or any insecurities. It's okay to have fear or to feel uncertain. We are human beings, and that's what we do. The key part is not to allow fear or the feeling of being uncertain to hold us back. That is when it's dangerous. It's dangerous because, now, we have let the negative feeling to control our destiny and make us lose out on what's on the other side of opportunity! Ladies, I invite you to discover your true worth.

Don't miss what God has for you!

TRUTHS FOR THOUGHT

A Note For Rejection.

Look at it right in the eye and say 'Okay, good bye.'

Key

Rejection is nothing but a redirection.

A Note For A New Season.

There is a process in uncovering who you really are. This does not happen from one day to the next. It is like when you peel an onion, and the onion has many layers. Each time you uncover each layer, tears begin to flow. For each layer that you begin to peel back, you will discover the beauty and pain. We have to understand that not all of us have had a beautiful painted picture life.

We are not to be silenced or kept in shame for what we have experienced in life. Our life is completely unique, and there is no other person just like you. I challenge you to find the courage and use your life, your story, and your voice as a tool to impact others. Be bold to inspire others. Use your pain to heal and transform others. Use your beauty to empower others.

Prayer to accept God into your heart.

Lord, forgive me for my sins. I believe that You died on the cross for me. That You came into this world for me. I believe that You have created me for a purpose and I ask You to come into my life right now. Change me, transform me, and show me why You have created me.

Father, I leave behind what I once knew to follow You. Give me a burning desire to know and to live for You. Show me the power that You have given me. Allow me to share my story to empower and impact others. Let this be the beginning of a beautiful journey with You. I trust in You, and I know that this walk won't be easy. But I want to go down this journey. I pray that You lead me to Godly women that will encourage me, lift me up, and pour into me Your love.

This prayer has made you a new creation. Once we accept Jesus Christ as our savior, we are washed clean from our past. We are new in his eyes.

THE HOLY SPIRIT

John 14: 16-18 (NIV)

And I will ask the Father, and he will give you another advocate to help you and be with you forever—17 the Spirit of truth. The world cannot accept him, because it neither sees him nor knows him. But you know him, for <u>he lives with you and will be in you</u>. 18 I will not leave you as orphans; I will come to you.

1 Corinthians 6:19 (NIV)

Do you not know that your bodies are temples of the Holy Spirit, who is in you, whom you have received from God? You are not your own;

Our bodies were created to have the Holy Spirit live in us. It is not until we become born again and accept Jesus into our hearts that we are able to receive the Holy Spirit. Before accepting Jesus, we could not see the Holy Spirit, but he is always at work. Even right now as you read this book, he is at work. Somehow, you came across this book and are reading my personal story in which I have prayed to make a difference in your life. I continue to pray that you may be awakened to the beautiful life we have been given. Today, you can decide to live a life that is spirit filled — filled with the power of the Holy Spirit who can dwell in you and perform even greater things.

John 14:12 (NIV)

Very truly I tell you, whoever believes in me will do the works I have been doing, and they <u>will do even greater things</u> than these because I am going to the Father.

1 Corinthians 2:12, 13 (NLT)

[12] And we have received God's Spirit (not the world's spirit), so we can know the wonderful things God has freely given us.

[13] When we tell you these things, we do not use words that come from human wisdom. Instead, we speak words given to us by the Spirit, using the Spirit's words to explain spiritual truths.

Luke 12:12 (NIV)

for the Holy Spirit will teach you at that time what you should say."

1 John 2:27 (ESV)

But the anointing that you received from him abides in you, and you have no need that anyone should teach you. But as his anointing teaches you about everything, and is true, and is no lie—just as it has taught you, abide in him.

John 14:26 (NIV)

But the Advocate, the Holy Spirit, whom the Father will send in my name, will teach you all things and will remind you of everything I have said to you.

Isaiah 11:2 (NIV)

The Spirit of the LORD will rest on him—the Spirit of wisdom and of understanding, the Spirit of counsel and of might, the Spirit of the knowledge and fear of the LORD

John 16:13 (NIV)

But when he, the Spirit of truth, comes, he will guide you into all the truth. He will not speak on his own; he will speak only what he hears, and he will tell you what is yet to come.

I highly recommend that after reading this book, you connect with a local church that can take you deeper into knowing who the Holy Spirit is. I have also created a curriculum called Shaped. In this curriculum, I walk you through the basics of what it means to follow Christ and go a little deeper into the works of the Holy Spirit. You may also go online and find books and studies that will also walk you through the basics of the Holy Spirit.

SCRIPTURES ON YOUR WORTH

Proverbs 3:15 (NIV)

She is more precious than rubies; nothing you desire can compare with her.

Song of Solomon 4:7 (NCV)

My darling, everything about you is beautiful, and there is nothing at all wrong with you

Psalms 139: 13, 14 (NLT)

You made all the delicate, inner parts of my body and knit me together in my mother's womb. Thank you for making me so wonderfully complex! Your workmanship is marvelous—how well I know it.

So God created man in His own image, in the image and likeness of God He created him; male and female He created them. [Col. 3:9, 10; James 3:8, 9.]

Genesis 1:27 (AMPC)

And, "I will be a Father to you, and you will be my sons and daughters, says the Lord Almighty." (2 Cor. 6:18)

For in Christ Jesus you are all sons (and daughters) of God, through faith. (Gal. 3:26)

What bigger satisfaction can you have knowing that you have been perfectly made, knitting together while being in your mother's womb. Created with value and worth. That you are more precious than rubies. There is no number that can compare to you. And there is no one with your same DNA, purpose or value.

#choose2bee

Join the movement.

Choose to Build, Empower, and Encourage yourself and others.

Connect with Joanna Esparza

Joanna is a dynamic, powerful, and enthusiastic speaker. She carries an anointing to speak not only to the youth, but to all generations. Joanna has a heart for evangelism and a desire to see girls and women of this generation intimately know Jesus and boldly have confidence in their purpose and calling.

If you're interested in having Joanna Esparza speak at your event, please send us a message.

Email: joanna1.esparza@gmail.com
Website: www.joannaesparza.com

Made in the USA
Middletown, DE
04 November 2023

41870857R00059